Ships are usually large.

What is a ship?

Parts of a Boat

The mast is the tall pole that holds the sail.

The front is called the bow. It rhymes with "cow."

The body is called the hull.

The back is called the stern.

Motors, Engines, and Propellers

Some ships have gas or diesel engines. The engines turn propellers that move the boat forward or backward.

Raft

The simplest kind of boat is a raft. Rafts are usually made of wood. You can make a raft by tying logs together.

In some countries, people use rafts for fishing.

You can use a pole or a paddle to push a raft forward.

A canoe is a narrow boat. It is pointed at both ends. The canoe is open on top so people can sit inside.

Canoe

Kayak

A kayak is a narrow boat. It is pointed on both ends like a canoe. Kayaks are closed on top so water doesn't get inside.

You can paddle a kayak on a lake or river. You can even go down a waterfall!

People sit in the cockpit. A kayak can have one or two cockpits. The paddle has two blades.

Rowboat

Oars are used the row the boat. The oars are attached to the boat with oarlocks. Oarlocks hold the oars in place and help the rower push the blade of the oar against the water.

Rowboats are pointed at one end and flat at the other end. You use oars to move the rowboat. The rower sits backwards in the boat.

Rowboats can be made from wood, metal or fiberglass. The oars are usually made of wood.

Dinghy

A **dinghy** is a small boat. It is often carried by a bigger boat or towed behind it. Some **dinghies** are made from wood or fiberglass. Others are inflatable.

Usually you have to row a dinghy, but some have motors.

Sailboat

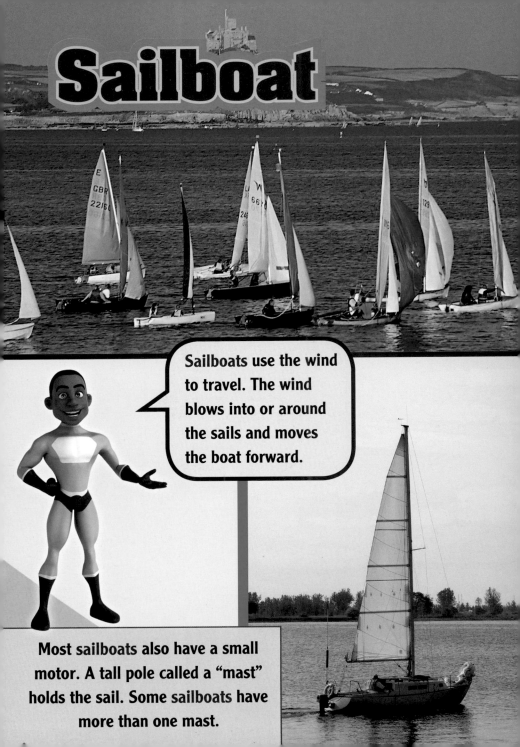

Sailboats use the wind to travel. The wind blows into or around the sails and moves the boat forward.

Most sailboats also have a small motor. A tall pole called a "mast" holds the sail. Some sailboats have more than one mast.

A schooner is a kind of sailing ship. It has two or three tall wooden masts. Schooners were more common 100 or more years ago. Some pirate ships were schooners!

Schooner

The Bluenose was a famous Canadian schooner. It was built in Nova Scotia in 1921. It was used for fishing and racing.

Schooners carried cargo across the oceans and on the Great Lakes.

Dhow

A dhow is a narrow, wooden boat with a triangular sail.
Dhows are used in the Middle East, Africa and India.

Dhows are trading ships. They carry food and goods for sale. The dhow is a very old kind of boat. People have used dhows for more than 2000 years.

Longship

Longships were Viking ships. They were used about 1000 years ago. These ships were long and narrow. They were made of wood, and they had oars and sails.

Longships were very fast. They could sail in shallow water and land on beaches.
They were pointed at both ends and could sail forward and backward.

A catamaran is a boat with two hulls. It can move through the water very quickly. The two hulls are joined by a flat deck or a larger structure. This is where the crew steers the catamaran.

Catamaran

Some catamarans are small sailboats. Others are large and have motors. They can carry people, cars and equipment.

The biggest ferry is Norway's MS Color Magic. It can carry 2700 people and 550 cars! Ferries open at both ends so cars can drive on and off. That way, the ferry doesn't have to turn around!

Ferry

A ferry carries passengers, cars and trucks. Some ferries even have railway tracks so they can carry train cars!

BC Ferries in British Columbia is the biggest ferry company in the world.

Fishing Trawler

A fishing trawler is a boat that carries big nets for catching fish. The nets are pulled behind the boat. Small boats catch fish and bring them to the port.

Big trawlers are like floating factories. They catch fish, cut them up, package them and freeze them.

Trawlers have special equipment for finding fish underwater. They have equipment for raising and lowering nets, and special storage areas for the fish.

Water taxis are small boats that carry passengers short distances. You can find them in big cities.

Water Taxi

Water taxis are like buses. They travel along a route and make regular stops.

Tourists often take water taxis. It's a great way to go sightseeing!

A fireboat is like a floating fire engine. It has pumps and water guns for putting out fires on ships and on land.

Fireboats pump water from the lake or ocean. They never run out of water!

A fireboat can pump more than 145,000 liters per minute. That's enough water to fill 1000 bathtubs! The fireboat's water guns can shoot water over 100 meters into the air. That's as high as a 25-storey building!

Fireboat

Tugboat

Tugboats are small but powerful. They tow or push large ships into harbors. Old tugboats had steam engines. Modern tugboats have diesel motors.

Some tugboats have firefighting equipment so they can help put out fires on ships or on shore. Tugboats also help move rafts of logs, oil platforms, barges and ships that have broken down.

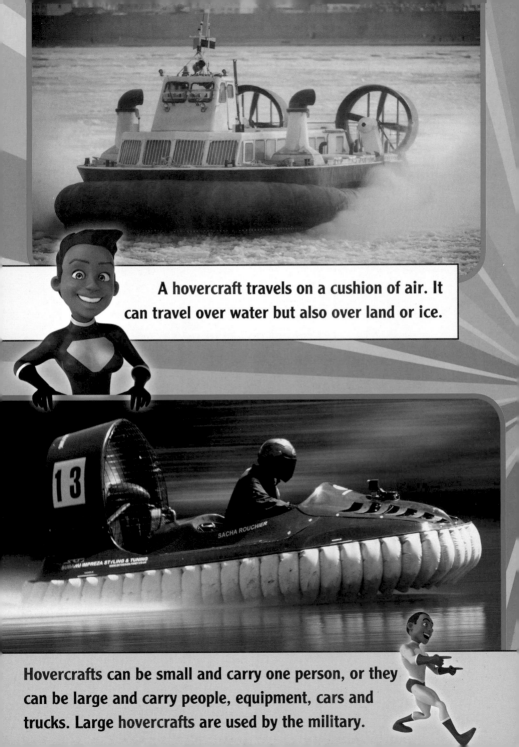

A hovercraft travels on a cushion of air. It can travel over water but also over land or ice.

Hovercrafts can be small and carry one person, or they can be large and carry people, equipment, cars and trucks. Large hovercrafts are used by the military.

Hovercraft

Hovercrafts have big engines that blow air under the hull. A skirt around the bottom of the hull traps the air. The fans at the back move the hovercraft forward.

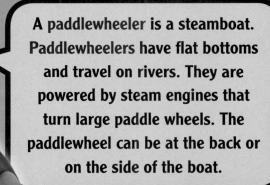

A **paddlewheeler** is a steamboat. Paddlewheelers have flat bottoms and travel on rivers. They are powered by steam engines that turn large paddle wheels. The paddlewheel can be at the back or on the side of the boat.

The paddlewheel is made of steel. It is turned by the engine. The blades on the paddlewheel push against the water. This moves the boat forward or backward.

Paddlewheeler

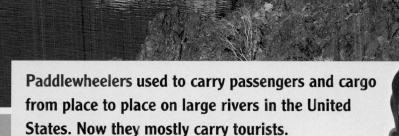

Paddlewheelers used to carry passengers and cargo from place to place on large rivers in the United States. Now they mostly carry tourists.

Icebreaker

An icebreaker has an extra-strong hull with a special shape. It breaks the ice and pushes it under or around the ship.

Icebreakers work in the Arctic or Antarctic. They often help other ships that get trapped by ice.

Ocean Liner

Ocean liners carried passengers across oceans 100 or more years ago. They were like cruise ships.

A famous ocean liner was the RMS Queen Mary. It is now a museum in California. Besides passengers, ocean liners also carried mail and some cargo.

The most famous ocean liner was the RMS Titanic. It hit an iceberg and sank in 1912.

Cruise Ship

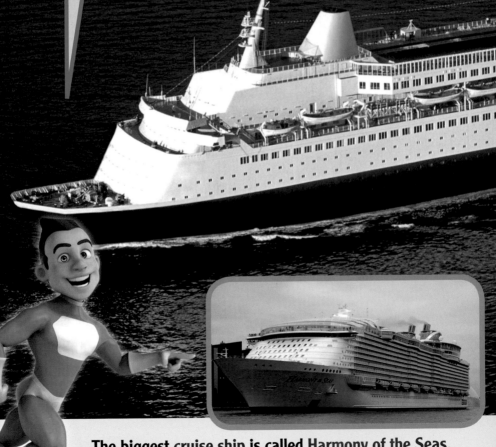

A cruise ship carries passengers.
They travel all over the world.

The biggest **cruise ship** is called **Harmony of the Seas**.
It can carry 5400 guests and 2300 crewmembers.

Cruise ships are like floating hotels. They have rooms for people to live and sleep in. They also have swimming pools, restaurants, mini golf, movie theaters and shopping malls.

OASIS OF THE SEAS

Yacht

Yachts come in many different sizes. Some are as long as a bus, but the really big ones are as long as a city block. They are called superyachts.

A superyacht can have a swimming pool, a dining room and four or five bedrooms. It might even have a gym or a movie theater!

Yachts are used for recreation. People use them to go on trips for fun. Some people may even live on a yacht!

Some yachts have sails.

Destroyer

A **destroyer** is a navy ship. It is a kind of warship. Destroyers are fast and can change direction quickly.

Some destroyers have tall, straight sides and complicated shapes so that they can't be seen on radar. Destroyers carry weapons such as missiles. Some have helicopter landing pads.

Aircraft Carrier

An aircraft carrier is like a floating airport. Supercarriers can carry up to 90 planes. Aircraft carriers are long and wide, so most travel slowly. Nuclear-powered carriers can travel much faster.

There are 37 active aircraft carriers in the world. They belong to 12 different countries.

Airplanes can take off from and land on the deck. Aircraft carriers can have crews of more than 500 seamen.

Submarines are boats that go underwater. They look like tubes with rounded ends. Some can stay underwater for almost three weeks!

Submarines have a tower in the middle that has equipment for communication and navigation. Ballast tanks filled with air or water help the submarine to float or sink.

Submarine

Some submarines can only hold one or two people. Bigger submarines have crews with as many as 80 people.

Submarines are used by the military and for scientific research.

Bulk Carrier

A bulk carrier is a cargo ship. It carries unpackaged, dry cargo such as grain or coal. It takes a long time to load and unload cargo, so the bulk carrier spends a lot of time in port.

The cargo is stored on the deck. It can also go under the deck in an area called the hold. The biggest bulk carriers can carry 400,000 tonnes of cargo. That's as heavy as 1000 big jet planes!

Container Ship

A container ship is a kind of cargo ship. It carries cargo in big boxes called containers. Larger container ships can carry about 19,000 containers.

Special cranes stack the containers on the ship.

Container ships travel about 40 kilometers per hour. That is slower than cars drive on city streets.

Oil Tanker

Oil tankers carry oil. Their hulls have double walls so the oil doesn't leak out. Most tankers pump the oil from their cargo holds into tanks located on shore.

The biggest are called supertankers. They can be 450 meters long. That is about as long as five football fields!

© 2017 Mega Machines

First printed in 2017 10 9 8 7 6 5 4 3 2 1

Printed in China

The Publisher: Mega Machines is an imprint of Blue Bike Books

Library and Archives Canada Cataloguing in Publication

Carrière, Nicholle, 1961–, author
Ships & boats / Nicholle Carrière.

(Super explorers)
Issued in print and electronic formats.
ISBN 978-1-926700-76-2 (softcover)
ISBN 978-1-926700-77-9 (epub)

1. Ships—Juvenile literature. 2. Boats and boating—Juvenile literature. I. Title. II. Title: Ships and boats.

VM150.C33 2017   j623.82   C2017-901951-1   C2017-901952-X

Frontcover: Container, ilfede/Thinkstock

Backcover: Barque, Kruzenshtern Zeglarz/Public domain-Wiki; Fireboat, Joshua Sherurcij/Attribution-Wiki; Hovercraft, Purestock/Thinkstock

Photo Credits: Ahmetgul/Thinkstock 50b; ake1150sb/Thinkstock 61; alexeys/Thinkstock 29; altrendo images/Thinkstock 14-15; Anton_Petrus/Thinkstock 26-27; antpun/Thinkstock 33b; basslinegfx/Thinkstock 18b; Brian Burnell 53a; CampPhoto/Thinkstock 13b; Czgur/Thinkstock 60; Dave Souza 59a; David Jones 46-47; Dikuch/Thinkstock 63a; Edward 34b; EkaterinaGolubkova/Thinkstock 9b; Etan Tal 30b; FamVeld/Thinkstock 8-9; ferrerivideo/Thinkstock 51a; FGO Stuart 46; Fletcher6 28b; Förderverein Schoner 20; GentooMultimediaLimited/Thinkstock 44b, 45b; Grafner/Thinkstock 5; Harno Thornycroft 34a; haveseen/Thinkstock 28a; Hilarmont 19a; IakovKalinin/Thinkstock 51b; Ifistand/Thinkstock 43b; iv-serg/Thinkstock 14b; j76n/Thinkstock 4-5; Jmabel 35b; JOC Peter D Sundberg 57; joelblit/Thinkstock 11a; Joshua Sherurcij 36b; Jupiterimages/Thinkstock 10-11, 48-49; karakoc/Thinkstock 6-7; Kees Torn 48b; Keith Skipper 60-61; KenWalker 31b; Kruzenshtern_Zeglarz 22-23; Lady-Photo/Thinkstock 38-39; Leamus/Thinkstock 44-45; leoaleks/Thinkstock 41b; leontudor/Thinkstock 62; LMGPhotos/Thinkstock 27b; marekuliasz/Thinkstock 11b; mariusz_prusaczyk/Thinkstock 25b; Mike Powell/Thinkstock 13a; Mike Watson Images/Thinkstock 19b; MR1805/Thinkstock 27a; mscornelius/Thinkstock 32-33; Muhammad Mahdi Karim 24-25; nevenmn/Thinkstock 7b; nightman1965/Thinkstock 2-3, 39b; PekePON 36-37; Pogli/Thinkstock 59b; Purestock/Thinkstock 40b, 55a, 55b; RaZZeRs/Thinkstock 40a; Remi Jouan 21b; riley 17a; RonyZmiri/Thinkstock 36a; Rootology 17b; SajjadF 25a; saoirse_2010/Thinkstock 6b; Schnaggli 31a; Sevaljevic/Thinkstock 50a; shunjian123/Thinkstock 9a; Stephen & Katherine 49b; Steve Mason/Thinkstock 15a; Steven J Myers 58; Streluk/Thinkstock 22; strevens/Thinkstock 41a; targovcom/Thinkstock 16b; tcly/Thinkstock 63b; temis/Thinkstock 42; Top Photo/Thinkstock 18a; uatp2/Thinkstock 56a; USNavy 52, 53b, 54-55; Vasilvich/Thinkstock 33a; Vipersniper/Thinkstock 43a; VollwertBIT 30a; ymgerman/Thinkstock 56b; zabelin/Thinkstock 12-13; Zoonar RF/Thinkstock 16a, 39a.

Background Graphics: IgorZakowski/Thinkstock 6–7, 16–17, 24–25, 26–27, 28–29, 30–31, 34–35, 36–37, 38–39, 42–43, 50–51, 54–55, 56–57, 58–59; iwanara-MC/Thinkstock 9–10, 40–41, 62–63; shelma1/Thinkstock 2–3, 22–23, 52–53.

Superhero Illustrations: julos/Thinkstock.

Produced with the assistance of the Government of Alberta, Alberta Media Fund.

We acknowledge the financial support of the Government of Canada.

$\mathcal{A}$lberta ∎
Government

Funded by the Government of Canada
Financé par le gouvernement du Canada

PC: 28